Traditional Irish Recipes

Traditional Irish Recipes

by

John Murphy

hand-scribed by
Margaret batt

WINGS BOOKS
New York
Avenel, New Jersey

This 1988 edition is published by Wings Books, distributed by Outlet Book
Company, Inc., a Random House Company, 40 Engelhard Avenue,
Avenel, New Jersey 07001, by arrangement with Appletree Press, Ltd.
Printed and bound in the United States of America

Library of Congress Cataloging-in-Publication Data
Murphy, John.
Traditional Irish recipes.
Reprint. Originally published: Belfast : Appletree Press, 1980.
I. Cookery, Irish. I. Batt, Margaret. II. Title.
TX 717.5.M87 1988 641.59415 88-8467
ISBN 0-517-67582-X

10 9 8 7 6 5 4

to Denise

CONTENTS

PREFACE

How old does a recipe have to be before it is traditional. by any standards all in this book are old enough — with perhaps the exception of Irish coffee — and all it needs is time —

Many were collected from friends & relations who in the nature of things had them from their mothers & they from their mothers before them

Others were recorded in dusty volumes such as 'the compleat confectioner, or the whole art of confectionary made plain &

easy' (h. glasse, dublin 1742)
or 'the lady's assistant
for regulating and supply-
ing her table' (charlotte
mason, dublin 1778)

✻ not that all the titles
have such charm, for ex-
ample the condescending
tone of J. mcwater's recipe
for soyer's soup is herald-
ed in the name of his book
'cheap recipes & hints on
cookery collected for dis-
tribution amongst the
irish peasantry in 1847'.
In this & one or two other
cases I have preserved the
language of the original
but most have been written
in a more or less uniform
style.

✽ The recipes themselves
cover the country with
yellowman from bally-
castle in the north to
drisheen from Cork, taking
in on the way grunt soup
from the southern shores
of lough neagh and gur
cake & coddle from dublin.
✽ I hope you enjoy cook-
ing and eating them as
much as I have collecting
them ⁓⁓⁓⁓⁓⁓⁓⁓

Traditional Irish Recipes

boxty in the pan

1 tsp. salt
1 lb. flour
1 tsp. baking soda
1 lb. raw potatoes
1 lb. mashed potatoes
buttermilk

Peel the raw potatoes & grate them onto a linen teatowel. Squeeze and collect the liquid in a basin, & leave to stand. Mix the grated potatoes & the mashed potatoes. When the starch has separated from the liquid pour off the water and add the starch to the potatoes. Add the dry ingredients and mix well, then add enough buttermilk to form a dropping consistency. Beat well & leave to stand a little before frying in spoonfuls in a greased pan. Fry on both sides & serve with butter & sugar.

barm brack

salt
2 eggs
1 lb. flour
2 oz. butter
½ lb. sultanas
½ lb. currants
¾ oz. yeast
½ pt. milk [warmed]
2 tblsp. sugar
4 oz. mixed peel
ground cinnamon
grated nutmeg

Sift the flour together with the spices and a pinch of salt, then rub in the butter. Cream the yeast with half the sugar and a little milk. Mix the rest of the sugar into the flour, add the warmed milk, eggs & yeast, and beat well. Fold in the fruit and the mixed peel. Turn into an eight inch buttered cake (over)

(over)

tin, cover with a cloth and leave in a warm place to rise for about an hour, or until it has doubled in size. brush the top with a little beaten egg. bake near the top of a hot oven for one hour.

boxty on the griddle

1 tsp. salt
¼ lb. flour
1 lb. raw potatoes
1 lb. mashed potatoes

Proceed as for 'boxty in the pan' adding enough flour to make a workable dough. knead a little, then roll out and cut into farls. bake on a hot griddle & serve warm with butter.

tripe and onions

1 pt. milk
1 lb. tripe
chopped parsley
1 lb. onions
1 oz. flour &
1 oz. butter
blended together

Cut the tripe into two inch squares bring to the boil three times in fresh water. slice the onions. add the tripe & the milk. season and simmer over a low fire for about two hours. Thicken the liquid with the flour and butter. add seasoning and serve sprinkled with parsley.

cockle soup

parsley
stick of celery
1 oz. flour
1 oz. butter
1 quart cockles
1 pt. water
1 pt. milk

COVER the cockles with cold water and boil until they open. Shell them, removing the beards, & keep the liquor. Make a roux with the flour and butter. Blend in the liquor and the milk, add the chopped celery and simmer for half an hour. Return the cockles, & add the chopped parsley. Cook gently for a few minutes. Serve

Yellow Man

1 lb. syrup
¼ lb. butter
1 lb. brown sugar
1 tsp. baking soda
2 tsp. vinegar

Dissolve the sugar, butter, syrup and vinegar, then boil without stirring until a drop hardens in cold water. Remove from the heat and quickly stir in the soda which will foam up. Pour into a greased tin to cool & break into chunks. Store in an airtight tin

willicks
sea water
1 pt. willicks or winkles

Cover the willicks with sea water. boil for ten minutes. Eat with a pin when cool. ॐ

Take the fish, scale, remove the head, fins, and gut them. Wash & pat dry, then toss in seasoned flour. Fry rapidly on both sides until the skin is crisp. Continue frying for a further five minutes or until cooked. ॐ

herrings
salt & pepper
flour
fried herrings

Carrigeen Moss Blancmange

lemon rind
1½ pt. milk
2 tblsp. sugar
½ oz. carrigeen moss

Wash the moss. Place in a saucepan with milk and lemon rind. Bring slowly to the boil & add the sugar. Strain into a wetted mould. Turn out when set and serve with stewed fruit.

brotchán foltchep

parsley
2 lb. leeks
2 pt. milk
knob of butter
2 oz. oatmeal
salt & pepper

oil the milk with the oatmeal until cooked. add the butter and mix in the chopped leeks. ∴ ∴ Cool gently for one hour. Season to taste & garnish with chopped parsley. ∴ ∴

a pot of tea

water
milk
good quality tea
sugar

Bring freshly drawn water to the boil in a kettle. Use a little to warm a 1½ pt. earthenware teapot. Empty the pot, then add 3-4 teaspoons of good tea. Bring the kettle back to the boil. Pour the boiling water into the pot, then stir once. Cover the teapot with a cosy and let it brew for five minutes. Serve with milk & sugar.

guinness cake

4 eggs
1 lb. flour
1 lb. sugar
1½ lb. dried fruit
1 tsp. baking soda
½ lb. butter
¼ lb. cherries
¼ lb. mixed peel
¼ lb. almonds
pinch nutmeg
1 bottle guinness
1 lemon

Rub the butter into the flour. mix well with the dry ingredients. add the guinness, lemon juice & beaten eggs. bake in an 8 inch tin in a slow oven for about three hours.

25

buttermilk pancakes

1 egg
1 lb. flour
1 tsp. baking soda
large pinch of salt
1 pt. buttermilk
2 oz sugar

Mix the dry ingredients. add the egg & enough buttermilk to make a batter of a dropping consistency. Fry in spoonfuls on a hot greased griddle. Serve warm with butter and jam for tea.

Drisheen

2 pt. milk
1 pt. water
2 pt. sheep's blood
¼ lb. breadcrumbs
1 lb. mutton suet
2 tsp. salt

Strain the blood and mix with all the other ingredients in a basin allow to stand for one hour. Cover well & simmer for about three quarters of an hour. Cut into pieces and serve hot.

donegal pie

½ lb. bacon
2 hardboiled eggs
2 lb. mashed potatoes
½ lb. pastry

Grease a pie dish & half fill it with potatoes. Slice the eggs & place on top. Fry the bacon until crisp, then place on top of the eggs and pour over the bacon fat. Cover with the rest of the potatoes. Make a pastry lid and bake in a hot oven for about one & a half hours. Serve. ⚬⚬⚬

bookie's sandwich

butter
2 lb. steak
1 long crusty loaf
mustard

slice the loaf lengthwise and butter it. Fry the steak & place on one half of the loaf. & Spread with mustard and season to taste. Replace the lid and allow to cool under a light weight. Cut into slices when cool. Keep wrapped until ready to eat.

scones

1 egg
½ lb. flour
¼ pt. milk
large pinch salt
1 tsp. baking powder
2 oz. sugar
¼ lb. butter

Sieve the flour, baking powder and salt. Rub in the butter & mix in the sugar. beat egg & milk together. add to form a loose dough & knead lightly, flattening out to about half an inch thick. Cut into scones with a round cutter. bake at the top of a hot oven for about fifteen minutes. ° Serve hot for preference.

black caps

½ lb. sugar
18 pippins
2 tblsp. orange flower water
juice & rind of a lemon

Halve the apples. ∴ Set them together, cut side down, in a dish. Pour the lemon juice, rind and orange flower water over the apples. Sprinkle with sugar, and bake in a moderate oven for half an hour.

baked salmon

parsley
¼ lb. butter
1 whole salmon
½ pt. cream
salt & pepper

Clean the salmon & rub with butter. Place in a dish, pour the cream & chopped parsley over it, then season lightly. Cover & bake in a moderate oven (allow ten minutes per lb.) baste a few times.

mince pies

7 lb. suet
3 lb. sirloin of beef
7 lb. currants
2 lb. raisins
3 oz. cinnamon, cloves & mace
grated rind & juice of a lemon
& orange mixed
6 apples
1 oz. caraway seeds
1 pt. white wine
2 lb. sugar
pastry

STEEP the caraway seeds overnight in white wine. mix with all the other ingredients, having minced the beef, shredded the suet & chopped the apples. bake in pastry, made in the usual way in a moderately hot oven for about half an hour.

33

hare soup

1 hare
2 onions
1 red herring
½ pt. red wine
6 pt. water
3 oz. barley
salt

Take a large old hare & joint it. place with the other ingredients (except the barley) in a pot over a low fire and simmer for three hours. strain into a stew pan and add the already boiled barley Scald the liver of the hare, bruise it, rub it through a fine sieve, and add it to the soup. keep hot until ready to serve, but do not allow to boil.

pea soup

1 onion
2. pt. water
ham bone
1 lb. dried split peas

SOAK the peas over-night. Rinse and place in a pot with the coarsely-chopped onion. Cover with the water, add the ham bone and bring to the boil. Simmer until the peas are very soft. Remove the bone and serve

apple jelly

4 lb. sugar
a dozen cloves
4 pt. water
4 or 5 lb. apples
(good windfalls will do)

Wash the apples, and cut coarsely. Place in a crock with the cloves and cover with the water. Place in the bottom of a very low oven & leave overnight.

Strain the liquid through a jelly bag without squeezing. Measure the liquid and add 1 lb. of sugar for each pint. Dissolve the sugar and boil until the liquid gels when tested on a cold saucer. Store in clean dry jam jars &&&

Gur Cake

1 egg
2 oz. milk
2 oz. flour
½ lb. stale bread or cake
½ tsp. baking powder
2 tsp. mixed spice
pinch of salt
½ lb. currants
2 oz. brown sugar
knob of butter
½ lb. pastry

Grate the bread or cake & soak the crumbs in water for an hour, then squeeze out. Mix with the dry ingredients & combine with the egg (beaten) & milk. Roll out the pastry, cut in two & line the base of a 9 inch sq. tin. Spread the mixture evenly on top, and cover with the rest of the pastry. Bake for an hour & a half in a moderately hot oven. When ready (over)

remove from the oven and
sprinkle with sugar. Allow
to cool and cut in squares.

apple tart
water
1 tsp. salt
6 oz. butter
2 lb. cooking apples
12 oz. flour
4 oz. sugar

Sieve the flour and salt
and rub in the butter.
Mix to a pliable dough with
a little water, then allow to
rest in a cold place while
peeling & slicing the apples.
Roll out the pastry and line
an 8 inch buttered pie-dish.
Fill with apple slices and
sugar, & cover with pastry
lid. Cut a vent in the top,
seal the edges & bake near
the top of a moderately hot
oven for a little over half
an hour. Serve hot or cold
with cream.

Beef Wellington

2 oz. butter
2 ½ lb. fillet of beef
1 lb. ready-made puff pastry
salt & pepper

Season the beef & spread with butter. Roll out the pastry and wrap it round the fillet. Seal the edges by dampening them slightly. Glaze with a little beaten egg or milk and bake for about forty minutes in a hot oven.

Grunt Soup

flour
a dozen grunts
(the young of perch)
1½ pt. water
a knob of butter
scallions
salt & pepper

Scale and clean

the grunts. Cover with water and cook until tender. Take out the fish & remove skin & bones. Add chopped scallions and cook for fifteen minutes. Add the butter &, thicken with the flour. Return the fish meat and bring to the boil again. Season and serve

PORK CISTE

6 pork chops
2 pork kidneys
1 large onion
1 large carrot
mixed herbs
salt & pepper
½ lb. flour
¼ lb. grated suet
¼ pt. milk
½ tsp. baking powder
salt

Slice the kidney and the vegetables, then place in a pot with the chops. Cover with water & cook over a low heat for about half an hour. ⁂ make a pliable dough with the flour, suet, baking powder salt & enough milk to mix. Roll out on to a floured ⁂ board & place on top of ⁂ the meat. Cover with a lid, allowing room to rise Cook for an hour and a half over a low heat

47

Rabbit Casserole

dripping
1 lb. potatoes
1 lb. carrots
1 lb. onions
2 oz. flour &
2 oz. butter blended
1½ pt. water
chopped parsley
1 young rabbit (jointed)
salt & pepper

Colour the joints lightly on both sides in a little hot dripping in a pot. Add the vegetables, cut coarsely & cover with water. Bring to the boil & skim. Simmer over a low fire until tender (about one and a half hours) Thicken the liquid with the blended flour & butter. Add the parsley and season. Serve with the vegetables arranged around the rabbit, and cover with the sauce

Roast calf's liver

spices
calf's liver
strips of fat bacon
½ pt. cream

Lard the liver with bacon strips rolled in savoury spice. Fasten on a spit. Roast over a good fire, basting with cream. Serve with good gravy.

Syllabub

Beat the cream with the sugar. Add the grated rind and the juice of the lemon to the wine. Beat all together. Serve in glasses.

2 oz. sugar
1 bottle sweet white wine
1 quart double cream
2 lemons

43

pig's head brawn

mace
cloves
mixed herbs
peppercorns
2 onions
1 small pig's head & tongue
2 pig's feet

CLEAVE the head in two, remove the eyes, & brains and any gristle. Wash well & scrape where necessary. ⁚ ⁚ Scrub the feet well. Just cover the meat with water in a pot &, add the herbs & spices Simmer for six hours over a low fire or until the meat is very tender. Remove the meat from the bones & return to the pot and keep boiling to reduce the liquid.   Remove the (over)

44

skin from the tongue and slice. Fill a tin mould with the pieces of meat, packing well while still hot. If too dry add a little stock from the pot. Allow to cool with a weighted plate on top. When cold turn out & slice.

hot whiskey

2 cloves
1 tsp. sugar
1 measure of whiskey
1 slice of lemon

WARM a stemmed whiskey glass with very hot water. Pour in boiling water and sugar to taste. Stir to dissolve the sugar, add a good measure of whiskey, a slice of lemon & some cloves

nettle broth

scallions
2 lb. boiling beef
2 pts. nettle tops
a cup of barley
salt & pepper

cut up the meat. place it with the barley in a pot, and cover it with half a gallon of water. Simmer over a low fire for two hours. add the chopped nettles and scallions, and cook for a further hour. Season to taste.

black pudding

intestines
small onion
½ lb. oatmeal
½ gal. pig's blood
½ lb. bread crumbs
½ lb. pork belly chopped
salt & pepper

Wash the intestines well & soak in salt water overnight mix the ingredients together & stuff into the intestines. Form into rings and tie each end. Place in a pot, cover with water and cook over a low fire for about two hours. Eat cold; or cut in slices and fry, and serve with fried bacon and eggs.

CRUBIN
water
pickled pig's feet

Allow two pig's feet per person. Cover with water & bring slowly to the boil. Simmer over a slow fire for three hours, or until the meat is tender. Serve hot with soda bread.

❀ ❀ ❀

Soak the beans over-night. Cook the feet and split open. Allow them to cool & coat in egg & breadcrumbs. Dot with butter & grill, cooking the beans at the same time. Serve hot.

dried white beans
egg & breadcrumbs
butter
pickled pig's
feet

CRUBIN SUPPER

potato pudding

milk
mixed spice
3/4 lb. flour
2 lb. cooked potatoes
salt & pepper

Mash the potatoes well. Work in enough flour to form a pliable dough. Add salt, pepper & spice. Form into a ball and place in a greased pot oven. Make some holes in the dough with a stick & fill with sweet milk. Cover & bake on a fire for four hours.

Stirabout

1 tsp. salt
3 oz. oatmeal
2 pts. water

Bring the water to boil & sprinkle on the oatmeal. Add the salt. Simmer gently on a low fire for two hours. Serve with honey, butter or milk

Mix the oatmeal with the salt & hot water form into large flat cakes. Cook on a moderate griddle on one side until firm arrange around the fire until dry on the upper side.

hot water
1 lb. oatmeal
salt

Oatcakes

potato apple

apples
4 oz. flour
1 lb. potatoes
½ tsp. salt
1 oz. butter

Boil the pototoes, & mash well, making sure there are no lumps. mix in the flour and knead to make a pliable dough, but not too much as this will toughen it. Roll out into a circle. Cut the apples into thick slices & place on one half. Fold the other half on top & pinch round to seal. Cook on both sides on a griddle, until the apples are cooked slice around, peel back the top & add lumps of butter & sugar. Keep hot by the fire until the butter & the sugar have combined. Serve in slices.

mock goose

1 onion
1 oz. lard
1 pig's stomach
mashed potatoes
salt & pepper

SCRUB the stomach inside & out, soak in salted water and rinse well. Prepare a stuffing by chopping the onion and frying gently in the lard, then add to the potato & season to taste partially fill the stomach with the stuffing. Sew up and roast in the usual way, or with a little lard in a pot oven on a turf fire, for two to three hours, turning once. Serve hot

Irish Stew

1 pt. water
1 lb. onions
2 lb. potatoes
2 lb. breast of mutton
or gigot chops
salt & pepper

Trim the meat & place in the bottom of a stewing pan, add some sliced potatoes and onion, season with salt and pepper, and add the water. bring to the boil & simmer for about an hour. add the remaining sliced potatoes & onions, cover & simmer for a further hour. When cooked, serve on a hot dish with the potatoes & onion surrounding the meat

boiled brisket

1 carrot
1 large onion
1 small turnip
2 oz. barley
3 lb. boiled brisket
salt & pepper

Place the meat in a pot, cover with boiling water and add the barley. Simmer on a low fire for one & a half hours. Cut the vegetables coarsely and add to the meat. Continue cooking until tender. Serve the meat on a dish, with the vegetables arranged around it.

stewed eels

eels
white sauce
parsley

Skin and clean the eels, then cut into three inch pieces. place in a pot, cover with cold water and bring to the boil. simmer for five minutes, and then drain. add a pint of white sauce. Stew for three quarters of an hour add the chopped parsley serve

mutton broth

1 onion
2 carrots
2 leeks
small turnip
1 tblsp. barley
1 lb. lean neck of mutton
parsley
salt & pepper

Cut up the meat. Dice the vegetables. Simmer over a low fire in one & a half pints of water for about two hours. Serve hot.

champ

scallions
½ pt. milk
5 lb. potatoes
butter
salt & pepper

boil the potatoes

and mash well. chop the scallions and heat with the milk, then beat into the potatoes with a wooden spoon. Season and serve hot, with a large knob of butter in the centre of each plateful. Eat from the outside in, dipping each forkful into the melted butter

Irish Coffee

1 tsp. sugar
1/4 pt. strong
black coffee.
1 tblsp. double cream
generous measure of
Irish whiskey

Dissolve the sugar in the coffee in a warmed long-stemmed whiskey glass. Add whiskey to within one inch of the rim and stir. Hold a teaspoon upside down over the liquid, then gently pour the cream so that it floats on the surface. ∴ Do not stir, but drink the coffee through the cold cream.

Perhaps not quite traditional ॐ ॐ but give it time ॐ ॐ

58

Soyer's Soup

2 onions
½ lb. flour
¼ lb. leg of beef
tops of celery & leeks
peelings of 2 turnips
½ lb. pearl barley
2 gals. water
1 oz. dripping
salt & pepper

Fry the chopped onion & diced beef gently in the melted dripping. Add finely-cut vegetables. Stir over a low fire for a further ten minutes. Mix in the flour and the barley and add the water bring to the boil & simmer for three hours.

Tasted by numerous noblemen members of parliament and several ladies who suffered no ill effects & who considered it good and nourishing for the Irish peasantry in 1847.

Florentine of veal kidney

3 eggs
2 veal kidneys
½ lb. spinach
1 sprig of parsley
3 small apples, quartered
grated orange rind
2 oz. currants
¼ pt. white wine
sugar
salt
grated nutmeg
½ lb. puff pastry

SHRED the kidneys well, fat & all. Set in a dish with the other ingredients. Mix well, then cover with puff pastry. Bake in a hot oven for about three quarters of an hour

60

dublin coddle

1 lb. onions
3 lb. potatoes
1 lb. best pork sausages
2 lb. thick slices of streaky
or back bacon
parsley
½ pt. water or stock

Cut the bacon into two inch square pieces boil, together with the sausages for five minutes, then place in a dish. Cover with thickly-sliced potatoes, the onions and the water or stock. Sprinkle with parsley & cook in a moderate oven, or simmer on top of the stove for an hour.

stewed dulce

dulce
butter
milk
salt & pepper

Cut the dulce from the rocks at low tide. Spread on shingle to dry in the sun. Wash well to remove sand and grit. Place in a saucepan with milk, butter, salt & pepper, and stew for three to four hours until tender. Serve with oatcakes. ~~~~~~~~

potato farls

4 oz. Flour
1 oz. butter
1 lb. potatoes
½ tsp. salt

Boil the potatoes. mash well, making sure there are no lumps. mix in the Flour and knead until it is elastic enough to roll out, but not too much as this will toughen it. Roll out into a circle & cut into four farls. bake until brown on both sides on a hot dry griddle or strong frying pan. best eaten with two fried eggs and several rashers of good bacon

boiled bacon and cabbage

1 cabbage
2 lb. piece boiling bacon
water

Place the bacon in a saucepan. Cover with water and bring to the boil. Simmer for about two hours, or until tender. Remove the bacon, slice the cabbage and add to the water. Boil for about ten minutes, keeping the bacon warm. Slice the bacon, drain the cabbage & serve.

soda bread

1 lb. plain flour
¾ pt. buttermilk
1 tsp. bicarbonate of soda
1 tsp. salt

MIX the dry ingredients together, making sure there are no lumps in the soda. Add the buttermilk and mix well with a wooden spoon. Knead lightly on a floured board. Place on a baking sheet & mark the top with a cross. Bake at the top of a hot oven for three quarters of an hour, until the bottom of the loaf sounds hollow when rapped with the knuckle⟶ ∴ ∴ ∴

65

baked potatoes

butter
potatoes
cream
salt & pepper

Scrub the potatoes & cut a cross on the top of each. Bake in the embers of a turf fire or at the top of a hot oven for about an hour, until soft when squeezed. Squeeze & peel back the opening on the top. Add a knob of butter. Salt and pepper to flavour. Serve with a dollop of whipped cream on top.

pratie oaten

fine oatmeal
mashed potatoes
salt

Work the oatmeal into the potatoes to make a dough. Roll and cut into farls. Cook on a hot griddle. Serve hot or cold, with plenty of butter

67

spiced beef

1½ lb. salt
1 oz. saltpetre
1 lb. brown sugar
(moist)
6 lb. middle rib
rolled & boned
6 tsp. mixed spices
(thyme, mixed herbs, mace
nutmeg cloves and allspice
black pepper and bay leaves)

pound the herbs & spices together and mix well with the salt, sugar saltpetre and minced onion. take the beef, boned, rolled and tied up well, and place in an earthenware crock. Cover the meat with the spice mixture, rubbing it well in by hand for several minutes. Replace the lid. Repeat every day for a fortnight, turning the meat once a day. ⁓

68

To boil spiced beef

1 onion
3 carrots
1 small turnip
1 stick celery
parsley
peppercorns
6 lb. spiced beef
(as in previous recipe)

Dice the vegetables and place them in the bottom of a pot Place the meat on top and cover with cold water. boil (approx. 30 mins. per lb. and 30 mins. over). When tender take out and press between two plates with a weight on top. leave overnight

colcannon

butter
½ lb. cabbage
3 lb. potatoes
small onion
salt & pepper

Boil the potatoes, drain, & mash well. Chop up the cooked cabbage & mix in with the potatoes. Chop the onion & cook gently in butter until soft & mix into the potatoes & cabbage. Serve on hot plates with a well of butter in the middle of each mound.

70

Stuffed Pork Fillets

2 pork fillets
(about 1 lb. each)
mixed herb & onion
stuffing

SLIT the fillets lengthwise without severing the halves. Flatten them a little, using the back of a knife. Spread the stuffing on one fillet, and place the other on top. Truss with thread or fasten with skewers. ✿ Roast in a moderate oven for about an hour. Serve with roast and mashed potatoes, cabbage & a slightly thickened gravy.

71

Flummery
oatmeal water

Place the oatmeal in a broad deep pan, cover with water, stir, then let it stand for twelve hours. Pour off the liquid. Cover generously with fresh water, let it stand for another twelve hours, & so on for twelve more—pour off the water, strain the oatmeal through a coarse sieve and pour into a saucepan stirring continuously until it boils and thickens. Pour into dishes. When cold turn out onto plates & serve with either wine & sugar, beer & sugar, or milk. Cider and sugar is particularly recommended.

baked limerick ham

cloves
brown sugar
bread crumbs
water to cover
10/12 lb. centre cut ham

Soak the ham overnight. Place in a pot cover with water and bring to the boil. Simmer on a low fire (allow approx. twenty mins. per lb.) Remove from the pot & strip the skin. Press a mixture of breadcrumbs & brown sugar onto the fat. Insert the cloves. bake in a moderate oven for three quarters of an hour

Wheaten Bread

½ tsp. salt
½ tsp. bread soda
½-¾ pt. buttermilk
1 lb. wholemeal flour
mixed with white flour

Mix the dry ingredients together and add enough buttermilk to make a wet dough. Knead lightly and quickly, then place in a 7 inch greased tin. Cut a deep cross on the top with a knife, and place in a hot oven for forty-five minutes or until it sounds hollow when knocked on the bottom ∴∴